PRAYERS FOR PARENTS AND CHILDREN

PRAYERS
FOR PARENTS
AND CHILDREN

and

'Life between Birth and Death
as a Mirror of Life between
Death and a New Birth'
(lecture of 2 February 1915, Dornach)

RUDOLF STEINER

RUDOLF STEINER PRESS

Prayers translated by Eileen V. Hersey, revised by Christian von Arnim. Lecture translated by Christian von Arnim

Rudolf Steiner Press
Hillside House, The Square
Forest Row RH18 5ES

www.rudolfsteinerpress.com

First English edition 1943, Rudolf Steiner Publishing Company, London
Second edition, enlarged 1968, Rudolf Steiner Press
Third edition, enlarged 1983; reprinted 1988
Fourth edition 1995
Reprinted 2000, 2004

The prayers, originally published in German, are selected from *Wahrspruchworte* (volume 40 in the *Rudolf Steiner Gesamtausgabe* or Collected Works); and the lecture, originally entitled 'Das Leben zwischen der Geburt und dem Tode als Spiegelung des Lebens zwischen Tod und neuer Geburt', is from *Wege der geistigen Erkenntnis und der Erneuerung Künstlerischer Weltanschauung* (volume 161)—both published by Rudolf Steiner Verlag, Dornach. This authorised translation is published by kind permission of the Rudolf Steiner Nachlassverwaltung, Dornach

A catalogue record for this book is available from the British Library

ISBN 1 85584 036 7

Cover by Andrew Morgan, art by Anne Stockton
Typeset by DP Photosetting, Aylesbury, Bucks.
Printed and bound in Great Britain by Cromwell Press Limited

CONTENTS

Ich schau in die Sternenwelt –
Ich verstehe der Sterne Glanz,
Wenn ich in ihm schauen Kann
Gottes weisheitvolles Weltenlenken
Ich schau' in's eigne Herz –
Ich verstehe des Herzens Schlag,
Wenn ich in ihm spüren Kann
Gottes gütevolles Menschenlenken.
Ich verstehe nichts vom Sternenglanz
Und auch nichts vom Herzensschlag
Wenn ich Gott nicht schau' und spüre
Und Gott hat meine Seele
Geführt in dieses Leben;
Er wird sie führen zu immer neuen Leben
So sagt, wer richtig denken Kann.
Und jedes Jahr, das man weiter lebt
Spricht mehr von Gott und Seelenewigkeit.

Facsimile of Rudolf Steiner's prayer
'Ich schau' in die Sternenwelt—'
(see pages 58 and 59)

FOREWORD

Prayers for Parents and Children is intended as a companion for parents who are looking for appropriate prayers to accompany their children on their journey through childhood. There are verses for every occasion: words which the mother can speak for the incarnating soul as it prepares to be born, as well as words for after birth; there are prayers for very small children and for older ones; there are morning and evening prayers, as well as graces to be spoken at table. The context for *Prayers for Parents and Children* is provided by Rudolf Steiner's lecture at the end of the book, which gives an insight into the larger cosmic relationships in which the individual is embedded before birth, during life and after death.

Translating verses of this kind requires a special skill to retain the spirit and vitality of the original without sounding stilted and unnatural in translation. The beautiful translations by Eileen Hersey are as fresh today as when they were first composed. They combine a true rendering of the original with the flowing English speech patterns which make them a pleasure to speak aloud to the child.

Christian von Arnim

PRAYERS FOR PARENTS AND CHILDREN

2

LICHT UND WÄRME ...

Licht und Wärme
Des göttlichen Weltengeistes
Hülle mich ein.

LIGHT AND WARMTH ...

May light and warmth
From the divine Spirit of the Cosmos
Enfold me.

4

Gesprochen von der Mutter

VOR DER GEBURT

Und des Kindes Seele,
Sie sei mir gegeben
Nach Eurem Willen
Aus den geistigen Welten.

NACH DER GEBURT

Und des Kindes Seele,
Sie sei von mir geleitet
Nach Eurem Willen
In die geistigen Welten.

Spoken by the Mother

BEFORE BIRTH

And the child's soul
Be given to me
According to your will
From spirit worlds.

AFTER BIRTH

And the child's soul
Be guided by me
According to your will
Into spirit worlds.

GEBET FÜR GANZ KLEINE KINDER
gesprochen von einem Erwachsenen

In dich ströme Licht, das dich ergreifen kann.
Ich begleite seine Strahlen mit meiner Liebe Wärme.
Ich denke mit meines Denkens besten Frohgedanken
An deines Herzens Regungen.
Sie sollen dich stärken,
Sie sollen dich tragen,
Sie sollen dich klären.
Ich möchte sammeln vor deinen Lebensschritten
Meine Frohgedanken,
Dass sie sich verbinden deinem Lebenswillen
Und er in Stärke sich finde
In aller Welt,
Immer mehr,
Durch sich selbst.

PRAYER FOR VERY SMALL CHILDREN
spoken by an adult

May light stream into you that can take hold of you.
I follow its rays with the warmth of my love.
I think with my thinking's best thoughts of joy
On the stirrings of your heart.
May they strengthen you,
May they carry you,
May they cleanse you.
I want to gather my thoughts of joy
Before the steps of your life,
That they unite with your will for life,
So that it finds itself with strength
In the world,
Ever more,
Through itself.

8

GEBET FÜR KLEINE KINDER,
DIE SCHON SELBST BETEN

Vom Kopf bis zum Fuss
Bin ich Gottes Bild,
Vom Herzen bis in die Hände
Fühl ich Gottes Hauch.
Sprech ich mit dem Mund,
Folg ich Gottes Willen.
Wenn ich Gott erblick'
Überall, in Mutter, Vater,
In allen lieben Menschen,
In Tier und Blume,
In Baum und Stein,
Gibt Furcht mir nichts,
Nur Liebe zu allem,
Was um mich ist.

PRAYER FOR LITTLE CHILDREN
WHO THEMSELVES ALREADY PRAY*

From my head to my feet
I am the image of God.
From my heart to my hands
I feel the breath of God.
When I speak with my mouth
I follow God's will.
When I behold God
Everywhere, in mother, father,
In all dear people,
In beast and flower,
In tree and stone,
Nothing brings fear,
But love to all
That is around me.

* Not to be taught specially. An adult says it every evening; the child gradually repeats individual words, then lines, and so learns the whole prayer.

10

GEBET FÜR KINDER ÜBER NEUN JAHRE

Seh ich die Sonne,
Denk ich Gottes Geist.
Rühr ich die Hand,
Lebt in mir Gottes Seele.
Mach ich einen Schritt,
Wandelt in mir Gottes Wille.
Und wenn einen Menschen ich sehe,
Lebt Gottes Seele in ihm.
Und so lebt sie auch
In Tier und Pflanze und Stein.
Nimmer Furcht kann mich erreichen,
Wenn ich denke Gottes Geist,
Wenn ich lebe Gottes Seele,
Wenn ich wandel in Gottes Willen.

PRAYER FOR CHILDREN OVER NINE YEARS OLD

When I see the sun,
I think God's spirit.
When I use my hand,
God's soul lives in me.
When I take a step,
God's will walks in me.
And when I see other people,
God's soul lives in them.
And so it lives, too,
In beast and plant and stone.
Fear can never reach me
When I think God's spirit,
When I live God's soul,
When I walk in God's will.

In one manuscript the word 'thank' takes the place of 'think' in the second and twelfth lines.

UM MICH LEBEN VIELE WESEN ...

Um mich leben viele Wesen,
Um mich sind viele Dinge,
In meinem Herzen auch—
Spricht Gott zur Welt.
Und spricht am besten,
Wenn ich lieben kann
Alle Wesen, alle Menschen.

ES LEBEN DIE PFLANZEN ...

Es leben die Pflanzen
In Sonnenlichtes Kraft.
Es wirken die Menschenleiber
In Seelenlichtes Macht.
Und was der Pflanze
Der Sonne Himmelslicht,
Das ist dem Menschenleibe
Das Geistes-Seelenlicht.

ROUND ME MANY BEINGS LIVE ...

Round me many beings live,
Round me there are many things,
Also in my heart—
God speaks to the world.
And he speaks best,
When I can love
Everything and everyone.

THE PLANTS ARE ALIVE ...

The plants are alive
In the sunlight's strength.
Human bodies are at work
In the soul-light's power.
What the sunlight of heaven
Is to the plant,
So to man's body
Is the spirit's soul-light.

MORGENGEBET

Sonne, du leuchtest über meinem Haupte,
Sterne, ihr scheinet über Feld und Stadt,
Tiere, ihr reget und beweget euch auf der Erdenmutter,
Pflanzen, ihr lebet durch die Erd- und Sonnenkraft.
Steine, ihr festigt Tier und Pflanze
Und mich, den Menschen,
Dem des Gottes Macht
Lebt in Kopf und Herz,
Der mit Gottes Kraft
Durchwandelt die Welt.

MORNING PRAYER

Sun, you cast your light above my head,
Stars, you shine over field and town,
Beasts, you stir and move on Mother Earth,
Plants, you live by strength of Earth and Sun,
Stones, you give firmness to beast and plant
And to me, the human being,
In whose head and heart
Lives the power of God,
And who walks through the world
With the strength of God.

ABENDGEBET

Mein Herz dankt,
Dass mein Auge sehen darf,
Dass mein Ohr hören darf,
Dass ich wachend fühlen darf
In Mutter und Vater,
In allen lieben Menschen,
In Sternen und Wolken:
Gottes Licht,
Gottes Liebe,
Gottes Sein,
Die mich Schlafend
Leuchtend
Liebend
Gnadespendend schützen.

EVENING PRAYER

My heart gives thanks
That my eye may see,
That my ear may hear,
That, waking, I may feel
In mother and father,
In all dear people,
In stars and clouds:
The Light of God,
The Love of God,
The Being of God,
Which, when I sleep,
Shining,
Loving,
Bestowing grace,
Protect me.

DER SONNE LICHT ...

Der Sonne Licht
Es hellt den Tag
Nach finstrer Nacht:
Der Seele Kraft,
Sie ist erwacht
Aus Schlafes Ruh':
Du meine Seele,
Sei dankbar dem Licht,
Es leuchtet in ihm
Des Gottes Macht;
Du meine Seele,
Sei tüchtig zur Tat.

THE LIGHT OF THE SUN ...

The light of the sun,
It brightens the day
When dark night is past:
The strength of the soul,
It has woken up
From restful sleep:
You, O my soul,
Give thanks to the light,
For in it there shines
The power of God;
You, O my soul,
Be active in deeds.

20

ES KEIMEN DIE PFLANZEN ...

Es keimen die Pflanzen
Im Erdengrund,
Es zieht die Sonne
Aus Finsternis
Sie in das Licht:
So keimet das Gute
Im Menschenherzen.
Es ziehet die Seele
Aus Geistesgründen—
Die Kraft des Ich.

THE PLANT SEEDS QUICKEN ...

The plant seeds quicken
In the ground of the earth,
The sun draws them up
From darkness
To light:
So quickens the Good
In human hearts.
The soul draws out
From spirit grounds—
The strength of the Self.

TISCHGEBET

Es keimen die Pflanzen in der Erdennacht,
Es sprossen die Kräuter durch der Luft Gewalt,
Es reifen die Früchte durch der Sonne Macht.

So keimet die Seele in des Herzens Schrein,
So sprosset des Geistes Macht im Licht der Welt,
So reifet des Menschen Kraft in Gottes Schein.

GRACE AT MEALTIMES*

In the darkness of earth the seeds are awakened,
In the power of the air the plants are quickened,
In the might of the sun the fruits are ripened.

In the shrine of the heart the soul is awakened,
In the light of the world the spirit is quickened,
In the glory of God man's powers are ripened.

* Rendering by A. C. Harwood

ES KEIMEN DIE WURZELN ...

Es keimen die Wurzeln in der Erde Nacht,
Es sprossen die Blätter durch der Luft Gewalt,
Es reifen die Früchte durch der Sonne Macht.

So keimet die Seele in des Herzens Schrein,
So sprosset des Menschen Geist im Licht der Welt,
So reifet des Menschen Kraft in Gottes Schein.

Und Wurzel und Blatt und der Früchtesegen,
Sie halten des Menschen Erdenleben;
Und Seele und Geist und Kraftbewegen,
Sie mögen sich dankend zu Gott erheben.
   Amen.—

THE PLANT ROOTS QUICKEN ...

The plant roots quicken in the night of the earth,
The leaves unfold through the might of the air,
The fruits grow ripe through the power of the sun.

So quickens the soul in the shrine of the heart,
So man's spirit unfolds in the light of the world,
So ripens man's strength in the glory of God.

And root and leaf and the ripe fruit's blessing
Support the life of men on earth;
And soul and spirit and the strong deed's action
May raise themselves in gratitude to God.
                    Amen.—

DAS LICHT MACHT SICHTBAR ...

Das Licht macht sichtbar
Stein, Pflanze, Tier und Mensch,
Die Seele macht lebendig
Kopf, Herz, Hand und Fuss.

Es freut sich das Licht,
Wenn Steine glänzen,
Pflanzen blühen, Tiere laufen
Und Menschen Arbeit leisten.

So soll die Seele sich freuen,
Wenn das Herz—sich wärmend weitet,
Gedanken lichtvoll kraften,
Beherzter Wille wirkt.

THE SUN ILLUMINES . . .

The sun illumines
Stone, plant, beast and man.
Our soul enlivens
Head, heart, hand and foot.

The light rejoices
When stones sparkle,
Plants bloom, beasts run,
And people work.

So should our soul rejoice
When our heart grows warm and wide,
Enlightened thoughts grow strong,
Enheartened will can work.

DIE SONNE GIBT ...

Die Sonne gibt
Den Pflanzen Licht,
Weil die Sonne
Die Pflanzen liebt.
So gibt Seelenlicht
Ein Mensch andern Menschen,
Wenn er sie liebt.

THE SUN GIVES LIGHT ...

The sun gives light
To the plants,
For the sun
Does love the plants.
So one human being gives soul-light
To others
When he loves them.

FÜR EIN JÜNGERES KIND

Vom Kopf zum Fuss
Durch Herz und Hand
Bin ich Gottes Kind,
In Sonne und im Monde,
In Stern und Stein
Fühl ich Gottes Kraft,
In Vater und in Mutter,
In allen lieben Menschen
Lebt mir Gottes Wille.
So will auch ich
Als Gottes Kind
Durch Gottes Kraft,
Nach Gottes Willen
Leben und sprechen
Und, was ich soll,
Gott getreu auch tun.

FOR A YOUNGER CHILD

From head to foot,
Through heart and hand,
I am a child of God;
In sun and moon,
In star and stone,
I feel the strength of God;
In father and mother,
In all dear people
God's will is alive for me.
So will I too,
As child of God,
Through power of God,
In will of God,
Live and speak
And what I ought
Do faithfully to God.

MIT MEINEN AUGEN ...

Mit meinen Augen
Beschaue ich die Welt,
Des Gottes schöne Welt,
Und danken muss mein Herz,
Dass es leben darf
In dieser Gotteswelt,
Dass ich erwachen darf
In des Tages Helligkeit
Und des Nachts ich ruhen darf
In Gottes Seligkeit.

WITH MY OWN EYES . . .

With my own eyes
I see the world,
The lovely world of God.
My heart must thank
That I may live
In this, God's world,
That I may wake
In the brightness of day,
And may rest in the night
In the blessing of God.

DIE SONNE SENDET ...

Die Sonne sendet
Zur Erde ihr Licht;
Der Gottesgeist,
Er strahlet hell
Im Sonnenlicht.
Die Pflanzen trinken
Das Sonnenlicht,
So wachsen sie
Auf Feld und Wiese
Und sind des Gottesgeistes
Geliebte Kinder—
Und Menschen tragen
Im Herzen und in der Seele
Den Gottesgeist;
In ihren Händen
Da wirket der Gottesgeist;
Ich liebe den Gottesgeist,
Weil er in mir lebet.

THE SUN SENDS FORTH . . .

The sun sends forth
To earth its light;
God's spirit shines
In sunlight bright.
The plants all drink
The sunlight in,
And so they grow
On field and meadow,
Belovéd children
Of the spirit of God—
And humans bear
In heart and soul
God's spirit too;
And in their hands
God's spirit works;
I love the spirit of God
Because He lives in me.

DIE SONNE SENDET ...

Die Sonne sendet
Zur Erde Licht;
Der Gottes-Geist,
Er strahlet hell
Im Sonnenlicht.
Die Pflanzen trinken
Das Sonnenlicht,
So wachsen sie
Auf Feld und Berg
Als Gottes Werk.
Und auch der Mensch,
Er trägt in Herz
Und Seele Gott.
Und seine Hände
Bewegen sich
Durch Gottesgeist.
Ich liebe ihn,
Den Gottesgeist,
In Herz und Händen,
In Sonn' und Mond.

THE SUN SENDS FORTH ...

The sun sends forth
To earth its light;
God's spirit shines
In sunlight bright.
The plants all drink
The sunlight in,
And so they grow
On field and hill
As works of God.
Man too bears God
In heart and soul,
And his hands move
Thro' spirit of God.
I love God's spirit
In heart and hands,
In sun and moon.

OBEN STEHET DIE SONNE ...

Oben stehet die Sonne,
Sie schenkt mir liebes Licht;
Im Lichte gibt mir Gott
Die edle Kraft des Lebens,
Und des Gottes Kraft,
Sie strahlet überall
In jedem Stein,
In allen Pflanzen,
In Tieren und Menschen—
Und wenn auch
In meinem Herzen
Die Liebe wohnen kann,
Dann ziehet Gottes Kraft
Auch in mich selbst hinein,
Die hohe Gotteskraft,
Die Christus den Menschen
Auf Erden hat geschenkt.

ES FREUET SICH DAS MENSCHENAUGE ...

Es freuet sich das Menschenauge
Am Schein der leuchtenden Sonne.
So freue die Seele sich auch
Am Gottesgeiste, der in allem lebt
Als die unsichtbare Sonne,
Die jedem Wesen liebend leuchtet.

THE SUN STANDS HIGH ABOVE ...

The sun stands high above,
It gives me kindly light;
In light God gives me strength,
The noble strength of life;
The strength of God
Streams everywhere
In every stone,
In all the plants,
In animals and man.
And if in my own heart
Love also finds a home,
God's strength will enter
My own Self,
The mighty strength of God
Which Christ has given
To us, mankind on earth.

THE EYE OF MAN IS GLAD ...

The eye of man is glad
In the light cast by the shining sun.
So may our soul rejoice
In the spirit of God, who lives
In all, as sun unseen,
Casting its light in love for every being.

ICH SCHAU' IN DIE STERNENWELT ...

Ich schau' in die Sternenwelt—
Ich verstehe der Sterne Glanz,
Wenn ich in ihm schauen kann
Gottes weisheitsvolles Weltenlenken.
Ich schau' ins eigne Herz—
Ich verstehe des Herzens Schlag,
Wenn ich in ihm spüren kann
Gottes gütevolles Menschenlenken.
Ich verstehe nichts vom Sternenglanz
Und auch nichts vom Herzensschlag,
Wenn ich Gott nicht schau' und spüre.
Und Gott hat meine Seele
Geführt in dieses Leben;
Er wird sie führen zu immer neuen Leben:
So sagt, wer richtig denken kann.
Und jedes Jahr, das man weiter lebt,
Spricht mehr von Gott und Seelenewigkeit.

I LOOK INTO THE WORLD OF STARS . . .

I look into the world of stars—
I understand their splendour
If I can behold in it
God's wisdom guiding the world.
I look into my own heart—
I understand my heart's beat,
If I can feel within it
God's goodness guiding man.
I understand nothing of the starry splendour,
And nothing of the beat of my heart,
If I see not and feel not God.
God has led my soul
Into this life,
And He will lead it to ever new life:
So say all who can rightly think.
And every further year we live,
Speaks more of God and the soul everlasting.

WIE DIE SONNE AM HIMMEL ...

Wie die Sonne am Himmel
Täglich das Licht der Erde sendet,
So soll meine Seele täglich
Sich zu rechtem Tun ermahnen;
Dass ich werde ein ganzer Mensch:
Leib, Seele und Geist
Für Zeit und Ewigkeit.

AS THE SUN IN THE SKY ...

As the sun in the sky
Sends light to the earth each day,
So should my soul each day
Arouse itself to rightful deeds;
That I become a human being whole:
Body, Soul and Spirit
In time and in eternity.

MORGENSPRUCH FÜR DIE VIER UNTEREN KLASSEN

Der Sonne liebes Licht,
Es hellet mir den Tag;
Der Seele Geistesmacht,
Sie gibt den Gliedern Kraft;
Im Sonnen-Lichtes-Glanz
Verehre ich, O Gott,
Die Menschenkraft, die Du
In meine Seele mir
So gütig hast gepflanzt,
Dass ich kann arbeitsam
Und lernbegierig sein.
Von Dir stammt Licht und Kraft,
Zu Dir ström Lieb und Dank.

MORNING VERSE FOR THE FOUR LOWER CLASSES

The sun with loving light
Makes bright for me each day;
The soul with spirit power
Gives strength unto my limbs;
In sunlight shining clear
I reverence, O God,
The strength of humankind,
That thou so graciously
Hast planted in my soul,
That I with all my might
May love to work and learn.
From Thee come light and strength,
To Thee rise love and thanks.

MORGENSPRUCH FÜR DIE OBEREN KLASSEN

Ich schaue in die Welt;
In der die Sonne leuchtet,
In der die Sterne funkeln,
In der die Steine lagern,
Die Pflanzen lebend wachsen,
Die Tiere fühlend leben,
In der der Mensch beseelt
Dem Geiste Wohnung gibt;
Ich schaue in die Seele,
Die mir im Innern lebet.
Der Gottesgeist, er weht
Im Sonn'- und Seelenlicht,
Im Weltenraum, da draussen,
In Seelentiefen, drinnen.—
Zu Dir, O Gottesgeist,
Will bittend ich mich wenden,
Dass Kraft und Segen mir
Zum Lernen und zur Arbeit
In meinem Innern wachse.

MORNING VERSE FOR THE HIGHER CLASSES

I look into the world;
In which the sun shines,
In which the stars sparkle,
In which the stones lie,
The living plants are growing,
The animals are feeling,
In which the human soul
Gives dwelling for the spirit;
I look into the soul
Which lives within myself.
God's spirit weaves in light
Of sun and human soul,
In world of space, without,
In depths of soul, within.
God's spirit, 'tis to Thee
I turn myself in prayer,
That strength and blessing grow
In me, to learn and work.

ABENDGLOCKENGEBET

Das Schöne bewundern,
Das Wahre behüten,
Das Edle verehren,
Das Gute beschliessen:
Es führet den Menschen
Im Leben zu Zielen,
Im Handeln zum Rechten,
Im Fühlen zum Frieden,
Im Denken zum Lichte;
Und lehrt ihn vertrauen
Auf göttliches Walten
In allem, was ist:
Im Weltenall,
Im Seelengrund.

PRAYER AT THE EVENING BELL

To wonder at Beauty,
To watch over Truth,
To esteem what is noble,
To resolve on the Good:
It leads human beings
To Aims in their life,
To Right in their action,
To Peace in their feeling,
To Light in their thinking;
And teaches them trust
In the working of God
In all that exists:
In cosmic worlds,
In depths of soul.

Life between Birth and Death as a Mirror of Life between Death and a New Birth

Dornach, 2 February 1915

The point has often been made in our discussions that anyone who wants to understand life and existence cannot start from the premise that they are simple. I have often drawn attention to the complexity and diversity of the harmonious cosmos, of which human beings are an integral part, even if only for the reason that people are often heard to say that truth—and normally they mean truth concerning the highest things—has to be simple. People like it best if they are told that such truth about the highest things does not really need to be studied, but that we simply possess it without the need to acquire it.

Everyone—I have said this before—is willing to admit that they cannot understand the workings of a watch if they have not learnt how the cogs and the rest of the mechanism functions. Only as far as the great, magnificent and mighty workings of the cosmos are concerned do people wish comprehension without effort. The basic aim of the science of the spirit, however, is to permit us slowly and gradually to make real sense of the meaning of existence and life.

Today I want to add something to the things we have discussed previously, starting with concepts and ideas with which we are already familiar and with which we have often concerned ourselves. To begin with, we have to say from the standpoint of the science of the spirit that outer existence within which we live is maya, the great illusion. But I have emphasized that within a western world conception it cannot be our view that everything which surrounds us is illusion in the sense that it is unreal. Not the world as such which affects our senses, which we grasp with our reason, is maya; in its innermost being this world is true reality. But the way that human beings perceive it, the way it appears to human beings, turns the world into maya, turns it into a great illusion. And when through inner training of the soul we reach a stage at which we find the deeper foundation of the things which are revealed to the senses, which are subject to our reasoning, we will soon recognize the extent to which the outer world is an illusion. For it appears in its true light, as it really is, when we know how to supplement and penetrate it with those aspects which must remain hidden in our initial observation of the world.

It is precisely what makes human beings human, what gives them their dignity and purpose, that the cosmos does not treat them like immature children to whom truth is presented on a platter, but that it is taken for granted that they acquire truth through their own work—their life's work. In a certain sense the cosmic powers count on our help in gaining truth, they count on our freedom and dignity.

Now the whole of human life as it initially progresses between birth and death is maya, an illusion. It has to be an illusion because when we view the world only as external physical objects and events we ignore the other aspect of the world and of existence in so far as it affects the human being; we ignore the things which human beings experience between death and a new birth.

Of course one might well say that one can understand human life between birth and death simply by observing it. Why is the other side, the life between death and a new birth, necessary? But even that is a false conception for the simple reason that the life between birth and death is a reflection of the life between death and a new birth. The things which we experience in the life preceding our present physical life are reflected in the life between birth and death.

In order to understand this reflection, it is necessary to consider two further things. The first is that we observe certain stages, certain highlights in our life between birth and death and investigate how these are reflections of the life between death and a new birth. At the same time it is necessary to realize that the life between death and a new birth is connected to a much greater extent with the unknown worlds to which we refer in the science of the spirit; with the events which occurred—before the development of our earth—on what we call Old Saturn, Old Sun and Old Moon. These events on Saturn, Sun and Moon are connected much more closely with our existence between death and a new birth than with the life between birth and death.

We might even say that the life between death and birth is influenced everywhere and in all its aspects by those foregoing lives which we know as the past planetary lives of Saturn, Sun and Moon. The effect of the latter on our hidden earth life between death and a new birth is in turn reflected in the life between birth and death. Thus the life between birth and death is a reflection of the events which occur between death and a new birth; they, in turn, are influenced by events on Old Saturn, Old Sun and Old Moon.

We have to examine certain key points, certain stages of our earth life if we want a more detailed understanding of this process.

The first event which belongs to our life on earth is what in human physical existence we describe as conception. This is followed by the embryonic stage. Only then does the birth of the human being, his entry on to the physical plane, occur.

Now a peculiar circumstance is revealed to the science of the spirit. There is only one event in the whole of human life, in so far as it is spent in a physical body, which is solely connected with the earth, which is in a sense explicable purely from earth existence. That event is conception. Nothing in human life other than conception is fundamentally connected directly and exclusively with earth existence. I must emphasize the word 'exclusively'. Conception has no connection with the life of Moon, Sun and Saturn; the causes of the event which occurs with conception originate in earth life.

Because external biology, external science, is concerned in the main only with physical existence, and from its perspective considers everything related to the life of the Moon, Sun and Saturn as folly, this external science can discover the truth in the physical sense of the word only about conception. That is why we find, when we read works such as those by Ernst Haeckel, that they emphasize those aspects which relate the human being to the processes in other organisms, and that those things are dealt with which are in some way connected with conception. Compare what I have just said with external science and you will find it to be true. When physical external science investigates the processes in the human being it usually descends to the level of the most simple cells. Such cells, forms from which human beings too originate (they develop from the fertilized egg), did not exist on Old Saturn, Old Sun and Old Moon. They are to be found only on earth; and on earth the combination of cells takes place which is of such importance to external science.

This particular stage of our life is nothing but the reflection of a real event which takes place before conception and which is connected with human life. In the final period of our life between death and a new birth, but also at the time of physical conception, we are clearly in the spiritual world. Something is continually happening to us on a spiritual level and conception is nothing but a reflection, maya, of this happening. But the event which takes place in the spiritual world is one which occurs between sun and earth in such a manner that the female element is influenced by the sun and the male element is influenced by the earth. Thus the event of conception mirrors the interaction between sun and earth.

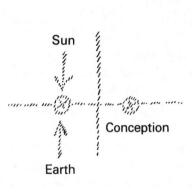

This event, which human beings frequently reduce to a level so degrading for mankind, therefore becomes the most significant of mysteries, the reflection of a cosmic event. It is of interest to draw attention to some details here. When a person approaches the time of his renewed entry to earth, a soul-like image of the parents through whom he will enter the earth is formed. How he comes to choose one particular set of parents we can discuss another time; this is connected with karma. But the thing to which I want to draw attention today is that the person progressing towards birth receives an image of the physical world primarily through the mother, he primarily sees the mother. He receives an image of the father—and I would ask you to consider this because it is important—because the mother carries an image of the father in her soul. Thus the father is seen through the image which the mother carries in her soul.

This is, of course, expressed in a somewhat simplified form, but it is essentially correct. These supersensory processes can only be put into words by characterizing them in their essential form. In order to prevent too fixed an image arising in your mind, I might add that if it is important for example that the soul and spiritual inheritance from the father's side plays a special role, if special soul and spiritual characteristics of the father are to be passed on to the human being approaching birth, a direct image of the father can also be created. But the image of the mother weakens to the degree that the image of the father is directly observed.

The next step of physical existence on earth is the life between conception and birth. This stage too—we call it the embryonic stage—reflects an event which takes place in the spiritual world before the aforementioned process. While birth in physical life obviously follows conception, that of which birth is a reflection precedes the sun-earth process which is mirrored in conception.

The existence of human beings between conception and birth can certainly not be explained from the conditions prevalent on earth. To try and explain it on the basis of physical forces and laws is pure nonsense, because it is the reflection of a process before birth which is essentially influenced by the remains of the sun and the moon from an earlier stage than the earth. It is a process which takes place between the sun and the moon, and thus it is in essence a spiritual one.

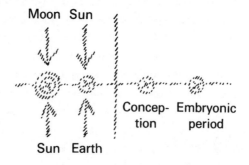

The forces which are active here are primarily those in play between the sun and the moon. Outer science has still preserved an awareness of this fact by calculating the embryonic period in lunar months, saying that it occurs over ten lunar months.

In this sense we have to take into account that in our life between death and a new birth we are subject to real influences from the sun and the moon. And that in our subsequent physical life we reflect this process, which is a sun and moon process, between conception and birth.

It should be noted that the term 'reflect' is used here in a somewhat different sense from the spatial one. In spatial reflection the object and the image are simultaneously present, but here we have the real process taking place before birth. The reflection occurs later in time. It is thus maya of a spiritual process before birth.

The next thing to take into account is the period between birth and that frequently mentioned important time in human life when we start to unfold our ego-consciousness, when we consciously start to call ourselves 'I'. This can be described as the real period of childhood. The period of early childhood—we can call it the infant period—is again a reflection of a process which lies even further in the spiritual past. The real process which is mirrored in the period when we start to babble without establishing the link between speech and ego-consciousness is a reflection of a process from before birth which extends even further into the cosmos. Here there is interaction between the sun and all the planets which belong to the sun, between the sun and its orbiting planets with the exception of the moon. The forces which are at play between the sun and its planets affect

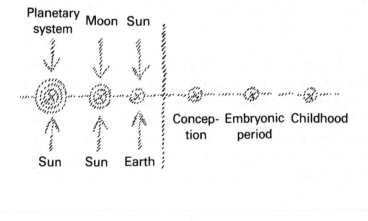

our life between death and a new birth, and what is created thereby long before our birth is reflected in the life of early childhood.

One can see from this that the child's life is affected by the reflection of things which are even further removed from physical existence than the moon. This has a deeply significant practical result; it has the result that human beings must not be diverted in this period of their lives from the forces which they receive and need to utilize. Consider the situation. Cosmic forces at play between the sun and its planets affect us before birth. These forces are present in the child which has passed through birth and has entered earth life. They want to emerge from the child. They really are in the child. In this sense the child in its innermost being is a messenger from heaven and these forces want to emerge. In principle we can do no more than allow them the greatest possible opportunity to come out. That is basically all that we should attempt to do on an educational level in the human infant stage: we should not interfere with the forces which are trying to emerge.

Such a view provokes a humble attitude. Whilst people normally believe that they represent a great deal to the child, the real point is that the forces which want to emerge should be interfered with as little as possible. Not that the educating adults mean nothing to the child—they do, because what emerges is a reflection which must be made real by the educator, which must be given substance.

Our task as educators can be shown in the following way. If we have a reflected object we have to fill the image with something which gives it more inward strength than it has purely as an image. Human beings are indeed born as reflections and they have to acquire the substance to make that image real. That is what their development between birth and death is all about. The reflections of the processes which we obtained from

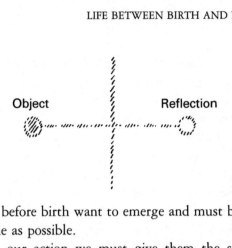

the cosmos before birth want to emerge and must be interfered with as little as possible.

Through our action we must give them the substance of reality; we interfere with them by giving them the substance of false reality by attempting to correct them. They are spiritual by nature.

Now you can understand the great significance of the consequences which arise from this. The person who brings up a child needs to have in his own soul, which has its existence alongside the child, supersensory ideas and feelings. For all purely material ideas and feelings which we bring close to the child interfere with his or her development.

The question is often asked how best to bring up a child. As with so many things, it is not a matter of setting up a few principles which we carry around with us to guide our actions. It is important that we start with ourselves, that we make an effort to carry within us a fund of supersensory ideas, that we are permeated by attitudes and feelings which enter the supersensory. For they have a far greater effect than what we can achieve through outer intellectual principles, through intellectual pedagogy. A loving mind which is at home in the supersensory world and thus deepens all feelings, thereby introduces a certain—please do not misunderstand this word—religiousness into the upbringing of the child. Such religiousness consists of loving a being sent from the spiritual world, of raising our love of the child into a spiritual sphere with the feeling that in extending our hands to the child we are giving him or her something as representatives of those forces which are not to be found on earth but in the supersensory sphere.

We can think up all kinds of educational principles but they will bear little fruit for as long as this science proceeds along materialistic lines. Only the things which are the result of the science of the spirit will bear fruit for the true education of the child. And the most important thing is the way in which we develop ourselves. In the outer, material world we may achieve much by what we do. As educators we achieve much more by what we are. This should be well noted and could well serve as a motto for good education.

Then comes the age of boyhood and girlhood, an age when we are still being brought up, but in a different way from the period of infancy. That is the next stage to be considered. It includes the whole period from the time when human beings consciously begin to refer to themselves as 'I' up to the point when they are released from education as such, when they freely enter life—the time when as well or badly brought up people they have to enter the whirlpool of life.

This too is a reflection, maya on a physical level, of previous events. The reality again lies between death and a new birth. Here the whole planetary system, from the sun to Saturn—or Neptune if we choose modern astronomy—is at work. The whole of the planetary system works together with the stars in the heavens, and the interaction between the stars and the whole planetary system becomes the forces which are active in us during the time of our upbringing.

So little of the reality of human beings can be explained purely from processes on earth that the only way to comprehend them during their upbringing is if there is a clear understanding that forces are at work in them during their life as a whole which are

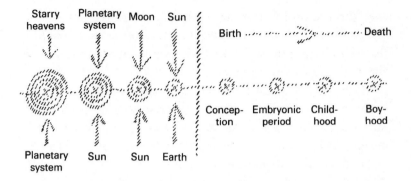

not on earth, which are not even in the planetary system but which lie outside the planetary sphere and work in harmony with the stars.

When we meet a child which can already call itself 'I', which we approach, therefore, in a certain sense as human being, we must be quite clear that something lives in him or her which is a reflection of something which is active not only outside our earth but outside our planetary system.

That is why the things which have been said about the early upbringing of the child are true in far greater measure for the following periods of education. Namely, that good education will only come about when it is drawn from the science of the spirit, when the teacher is aware that outside the planetary system a world exists which unfolds in the human being, and when this world is more than theoretical knowledge in the teacher and informs his feelings and attitudes and he himself has experienced the truth of this world beyond the planets. The unsure steps of such a teacher are often better than the ingenious educational principles of a materialistic teacher. Because insecure steps, actions undertaken in ignorance, can be improved in the course of our life. But what we do because of what we are does not correct itself during life.

It would be a good thing if the following were included

among the areas which would benefit from metamorphosis and change through spiritual science: an increasing understanding that those who want to become good teachers and educators—and that includes in principle all those who want to become parents—should do so through the assimilation of spiritual ideas in their soul. In order to become a good educator, the bulk of the work has to be undertaken on oneself. And it is more important for a teacher, for instance, to live whole-heartedly in the material to be dealt with in school the next day, before he enters school, than that he possesses the best possible educational principles on how to do this or that. After he has grown to love the subject, grown to live it inwardly in the spirit, he can even stumble in the lesson—although I do not want to recommend that—and he will do a better job than the person who enters school with all sorts of principles strait-jacketed into his brain and who knows everything about the most correct way to set about things.

We know that at present in the world things still take place the other way round. Those who want to be teachers today are tested above all for the things which they know, for the content of the knowledge they have assimilated. It is almost true to say that they are tested on the things which they can find in books, on which they can establish a library. The things which can be looked up in a library, if one has been taught how to do so, are the things which are largely examined. In teachers' examinations the important things ought not to be what the person concerned can easily find if he needs it, factual knowledge ought not to be the most important thing, but instead teachers ought to be examined in how in their attitudes, their feelings, they can establish a link with knowledge of, with feeling for the devel-opment of the universe as a whole. Attitudes towards human and cosmic development ought to be the yardstick for whether or not someone is a good teacher. Then, of course, those would fail the examinations who only knew the most facts and those would pass the examinations with flying colours who were good human beings in the spiritual sense.

That is also what will happen in the end. In the end we will have to move in the following direction: human beings who are not good, whose soul does not incline towards the spiritual life, will fail the teachers' examinations in future however much they know, even if they have all the facts that are required today at their fingertips.

This area in particular, then, will provide the opening that will permit less emphasis to be placed on intellectual knowledge and more on the development of the soul as a whole. Let me repeat: in such a situation our value will not be determined by the influence we wield in the outer material world but by what we do. As educators we are of value above all by what we are.

It is important that we take account of everything which is related to the reality of the process reflected in conception. All of that belongs to the earth. But in so far as it lies before birth it belongs to the interaction of sun and earth, it takes place in the earth's aura. A significant spiritual event takes place in the earth's aura preceding human conception which is reflected in conception. What takes place between conception and birth is in reality the interaction between sun and moon, and this is essentially a repetition of events which took place earlier during the Old Moon period of the earth.

In the embryonic period a real event is reflected which is like a repetition of the events which took place on the Old Moon. Similarly the process which occurs between the end of childhood, the point when human beings consciously begin to refer to themselves as 'I', and birth is a repetition of the influence of the Old Sun. The things which occur even before that, which are reflected in the period when we are educated, are a repetition of the Old Saturn stage of the earth.

And then, when our education is finished, and we enter the world well or badly brought up, what processes are reflected at that point? Then processes are mirrored which lie even before the Saturn period, which are not part of the visible world at all to the degree that they have no correlation in the outwardly visible stars. The correlations of our experiences up to the end of our educational period are still visible. They are yet related to the outermost stars which can still be seen. But our subsequent experience, our subsequent development belongs to the invisible world. We are released from the visible cosmos when we have truly completed our education.

And then, of course, it is a matter of enriching, or of having already enriched our soul with the truths of the supersensory worlds. That is the only way to find our true path through life. Otherwise we are puppets, guided by forces which are not meant to do so. The person who is free to enter the world after the Saturn stage has been reflected in his development, and has no idea in his soul of a spiritual world, is not in his intended element but is carried along by invisible forces as the puppet is carried along by the forces contained in the strings of the puppet master.

To assimilate what spiritual science can give means becoming human, means not remaining a puppet of the sensory world but achieving the freedom which is the element in which human beings should live and work throughout their lives. Indeed, freedom can only be understood in concepts which do not originate in the sensory world. For nothing that is given us from the sensory world can make us free. This is what I had in mind when I wrote my *Philosophy of Freedom*,* where I emphasized how— even without reference to the ideas of spiritual science—the foundation of ethics, of morals has to be seen in terms of moral imagination; that is to say, it has to be discovered on the basis of

---

* Published by Rudolf Steiner Press, London, 1979.

moral imagination, on the basis of something that is not contained in any sensory world, although of course morals should
not be considered as being purely imaginary. The whole chapter
on moral imagination is an affirmation that human beings
throughout life, in so far as they want to spend it in freedom,
have to recognize their connection with something which is not a
reflection of the sensory world but which has to arise freely in
themselves, which they carry within themselves, which is more
majestic than the visible stars, which cannot be gained from the
sensory world but only through an inward creative process. That
is the intention of the chapter on moral imagination.

These thoughts were again intended to show the numerous
contexts within which we stand in life. As the life before birth is
preparatory for its reflection, so the reflected image between
birth and death is in turn a preparation for the spiritual life
which follows between death and a new birth. The more we can
take from this life into the life between death and a new birth,
the richer the development of that life will be. Even the concepts
which we have to learn concerning that life, concerning the
truths between death and a new birth, these concepts have to be
different to those which we have to learn from physical maya if
we want to understand the latter. Some of the concepts which
have to be acquired for an understanding of the other side of life
as it passes between death and a new birth can be found in the
Vienna lecture cycle of 1914, *The Inner Nature of Man and Life
between Death and Rebirth*. It can sometimes be quite a struggle to
formulate, step by step, the concepts and ideas which are
required for this different life. And when you read such a lecture
cycle in particular, you will notice the struggle to find expres-
sions which adequately reflect these quite different conditions.

At this time in particular, when the deaths of dear members
are affecting our anthroposophical life, I want to draw attention
to one point. The occurrence of death plays a different role in the

life between death and a new birth than does the point of birth in our present life between birth and death. The time of birth is not usually remembered by human beings under the ordinary circumstances of physical life. But the time of death leaves the deepest impression for the whole life between death and a new birth; it is remembered above everything else, it is always present but in a different form than the one seen from this side of life. From this side of life death appears as a disintegration, something of which human beings have fear and dread. From the other side, death appears as the luminous beginning of spiritual experience, as something which spreads sun-like over the whole life between death and a new birth, which warms the soul with joy and which is repeatedly looked back on with deep and warm understanding. That is the moment of death. To describe it in earthly terms: the most joyful, the most rapturous moment between death and a new birth is the point of death as experienced from the other side.

If from a materialistic point of view we have formed the idea that human beings lose consciousness with death, if we have no real conception of the way consciousness develops—I say this particularly today because we are thinking of dear ones who have died recently—if we find great difficulty in imagining the existence of a consciousness beyond death, if we believe that consciousness fades because consciousness appears to fade with death, then we have to understand: this is not true. For consciousness is exceedingly lucid after death, and only because human beings are unused to living in this extremely clear consciousness in the initial period after dying does something similar to a state of sleep occur immediately after death.

But this state of sleep is the opposite of the one which we enter in ordinary life. In ordinary life we sleep because our level of consciousness is reduced. After death we are unconscious in a certain sense because consciousness is too strong, too overwhelming, because we live completely in the consciousness and need to accustom ourselves to this heightened state in the initial days. Then, when we succeed in orientating ourselves sufficiently to feel the emergence of the thought 'that was you!' from the wealth of world thoughts, at the point when we begin to distinguish our past earth life from the wealth of world thoughts, then we experience in this wealth of consciousness the moment of which it can be said: we awaken. We might be awakened by an event which was particularly significant in our life and which is also of significance for events after our earth life.

Thus it is a matter of growing accustomed to supersensory consciousness, to consciousness which is not built on the foundations and supports of the physical world, but which is sufficient in itself. That is what we call 'awakening' after death. One could describe this awakening as a probing by the will which, as you know and also can see from the above-mentioned lecture cycle, develops particularly after death. I spoke there of a feeling-like will and a will-like feeling. When this will-like feeling starts to venture into the supersensory world, when it makes the first probe, then it starts to awaken.

Those are things which, circumstances permitting, we will discuss further.

PUBLISHER'S NOTE

The lecture printed here was given by Rudolf Steiner to audiences familiar with the general background and terminology of his anthroposophical teaching. It should be remembered that in his autobiography, *The Course of My Life*, he emphasizes the distinction between his written works on the one hand and, on the other, reports of lectures that were given as oral communications and were not originally intended for print. For an intelligent appreciation of the lectures it should be borne in mind that certain premises were taken for granted when the words were spoken. 'These premises,' Rudolf Steiner writes, 'include at the very least the anthroposophical knowledge of humanity and of the cosmos in its spiritual essence; also what may be called "anthroposophical history", told as an outcome of research into the spiritual world.'